This book is dedicated to you – yes, you!
Anytime it feels like something is too hard,
I want you to say this sentence out loud:

**Dr Ronx says that I've got this, I can do it
and I will do it, and whatever happens, I tried my best.**

Special shout out to the kids of my chosen family:
Ada, Ahria, Bailey, Caelan, Chloe, Cooper, Darwin,
Eilidh, Emily, Fin, Grace, Harry, Josh, Kiki, Luke,
Maude, Marley, Noah, Oneicia, Oliver, Poppy, Tao,
Tyler, Wilf C, Wilf P, and last but not least, Zadie.
D.R.

For all the children and young people who will
read this book, I hope you get swept away
in the magic of art and education.
A.A.

First published in Great Britain 2023 by Red Shed, part of Farshore
An imprint of HarperCollins*Publishers*
1 London Bridge Street, London SE1 9GF
www.farshore.co.uk

HarperCollins*Publishers*
Macken House, 39/40 Mayor Street Upper, Dublin 1, D01 C9W8

Text copyright © Abidemi Ibironke Ikharia 2023
The author has asserted their moral rights.
Illustrations copyright © HarperCollins*Publishers* 2023
Illustrated by Ashton Attzs.
Photograph of Dr Ronx by Nina Photography.

ISBN 978 0 00 852089 2
Printed in Italy
001

A CIP catalogue record for this title is available from the British Library.

Stay safe online. Any website addresses listed in this book are correct at the time of going to print.
However, Farshore is not responsible for content hosted by third parties. Please be aware that
online content can be subject to change and websites can contain content that is unsuitable for
children. We advise that all children are supervised when using the internet.

Farshore takes its responsibility to the planet and its inhabitants very seriously.
We aim to use papers from well-managed forests run by responsible suppliers.

Always ask an adult for help when using paint. Wear protective clothes and
cover surfaces to avoid damage or staining.

Little EXPERTS

DR RONX

AMAZING BODIES

ILLUSTRATED BY
ASHTON ATTZS

RED SHED

INTRODUCTION

My love for the human body started with a fascination with plants. "What? Plants, Dr Ronx?" Yep, plants! Even though I am a medical doctor, it all started with a curious interest in plants.

One of the first things I remember being taught is that plants need carbon dioxide to live and we need oxygen. I thought that it was lucky that plants need our waste product (carbon dioxide) to survive, and we need their waste product (oxygen) to survive. And I loved the science experiments we did at school.

But why did I become a doctor? Well, not only did science excite me at school, I was always trying to find science and medical books in my local library. When I was older, I also watched a programme that was set in a hospital. I don't think I really understood much of what was going on medically, but I knew the doctors were helping people. There was a lot of blood, injuries and life-like operations. But not only this, the doctors were kind and caring. And there were doctors of all ages, abilities, races and genders.

In one episode, a doctor gave a patient a new medicine that enabled the patient to move a part of her body that had stopped moving due to brain damage. The patient was able to use her limbs and I was like WOW!

From that day, I made sure everybody knew I wanted to be a doctor. I studied hard to get the grades I needed and listened to advice from people around me. It wasn't easy and I had to make a lot of sacrifices, but my goal was clear. And a little-known secret is that I didn't get into my top medical school choice first time round!

Roll forward to today and . . . I am an emergency medicine doctor.

And with over 11 years under my belt, I want to share some things that I have learned along the way, so . . . *drum roll* – here is my ultimate guide to your awesome body: from your spongy brain to your gooey guts and lots more! I want you to become a little expert on the human body and wow your friends, family and teachers.

I hope you come back time and time again to use this book in your studies, for homework or just for fun!

Big love,

Dr Ronx

(they/them)

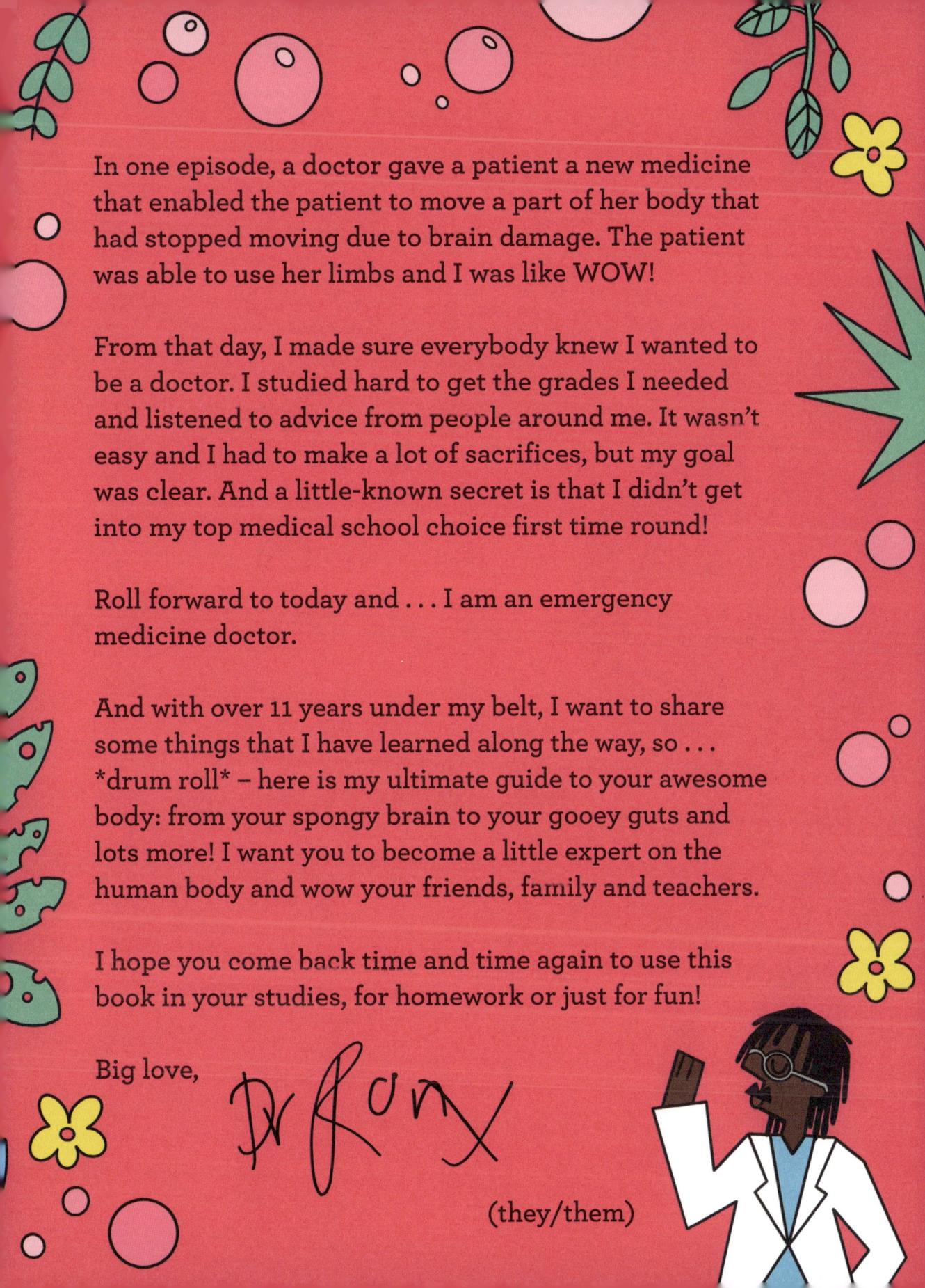

SUPER SKIN

Without skin, you'd see your muscles and bones (yuck!) ... and you wouldn't have earlobes and eyelids (terrifying!). But skin is more than a protective cover – it also helps control your temperature and shield you from infections and injuries.

Skin has different thicknesses. Thick skin on the soles of your feet helps you walk. Whereas lip skin is thin, so lips can change shape during eating or laughing!

Fingertip skin is unique. Ask an adult if you can dip your fingertips in paint and press onto paper. Compare to other people's. They won't be the same – even if you're an identical twin!

sweat gland

In your lifetime you could lose up to 35 kilograms of skin cells – that's about the weight of eight cats!

We lose and replace skin cells every two to four weeks. "Where do they go?" I hear you ask! Well, look around. Can you spot any dust? Dust contains dead skin cells, and not just yours but other people's too!

Skin is made up of three main layers. The layer we can see is the epidermis.

Grab a hairbrush and look for a whitish blob (hair follicle) at the end of a hair. Each follicle connects to a muscle in the skin that contracts when we are cold. This makes our hairs stand on end, which creates goosebumps.

Below the epidermis is the dermis. It contains blood vessels and nerves, sweat glands (to help your body cool down) and hair follicles.

muscle

dermis

nerve

subcutaneous

blood vessels

hair follicle

My skin is brown because of cells in the epidermis that produce melanin. The more melanin the cells produce, the darker the skin tone.

The last layer is the subcutaneous, which is mostly fat. It cushions your body and protects it from getting too chilly.

BRILLIANT BONES

You were born with about 300 bones. When you become an adult, you will have nearly 100 fewer bones. "Erm, where do they go?", I hear you ask. "Is it magic?" Well, not really – it's science!

Babies' bones are mostly made from cartilage. As a baby gets older, their bones harden and fuse together.

Can you feel the bone in your arm between your shoulder and elbow (humerus)? This was three bones when you were born, but began to join together when you were around three years old.

Hand bones

Ulna (forearm bone)

Radius (forearm bone)

The smallest bones are the stapes. They are in your ears and are smaller than a grain of rice!

Bones help protect important areas from damage. For example, ribs guard the heart and lungs.

Stapes

Skull

Clavicle (collarbone)

Humerus (arm bone)

Shoulder blade

Ribs

Vertebrae

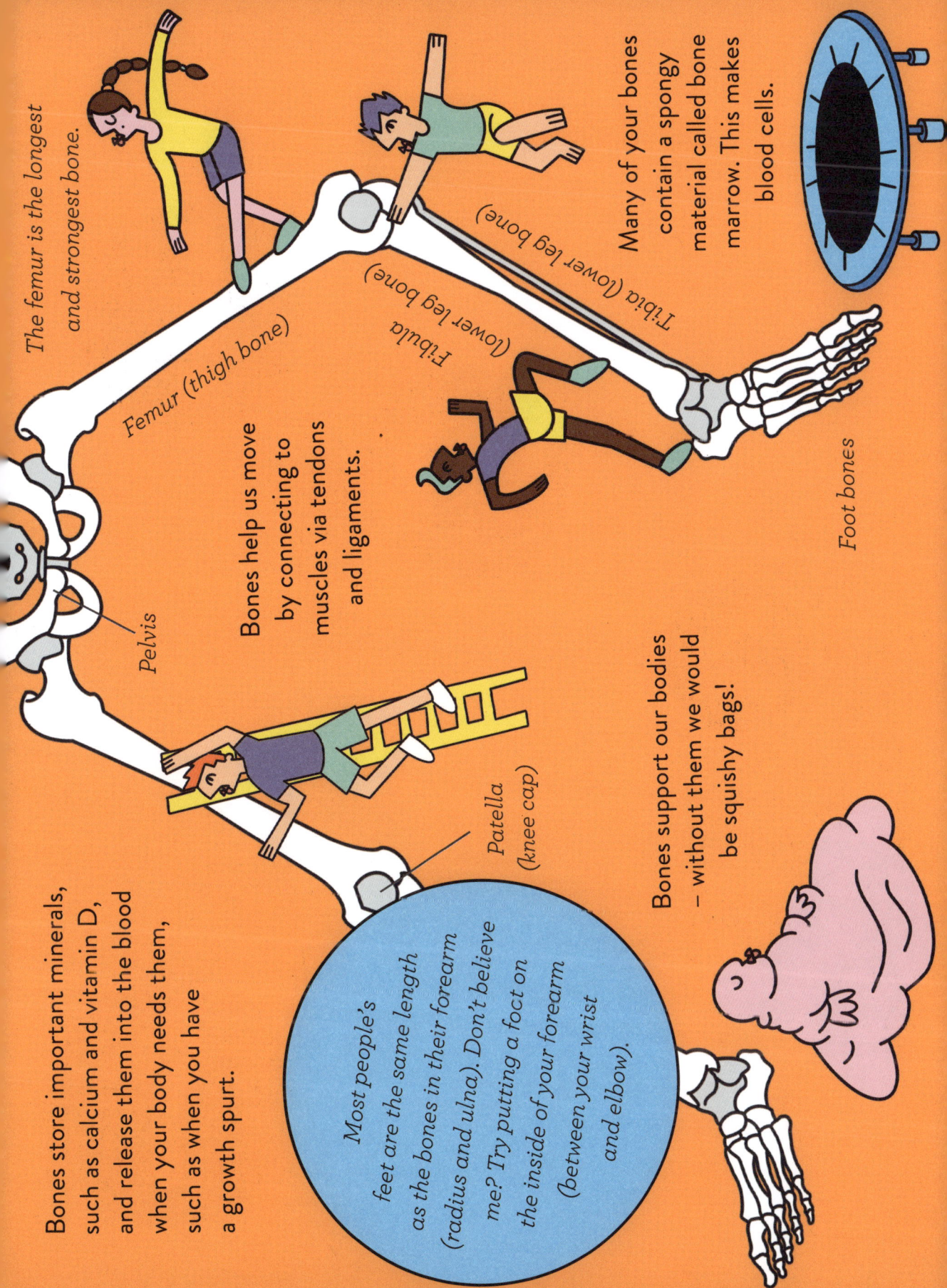

The femur is the longest and strongest bone.

Femur (thigh bone)

Fibula (lower leg bone)

Tibia (lower leg bone)

Many of your bones contain a spongy material called bone marrow. This makes blood cells.

Foot bones

Pelvis

Bones help us move by connecting to muscles via tendons and ligaments.

Patella (knee cap)

Bones support our bodies – without them we would be squishy bags!

Bones store important minerals, such as calcium and vitamin D, and release them into the blood when your body needs them, such as when you have a growth spurt.

Most people's feet are the same length as the bones in their forearm (radius and ulna). Don't believe me? Try putting a foot on the inside of your forearm (between your wrist and elbow).

TWIST AND TURN

Joints connect bones together and can help your body to move. You have nearly 400 of them and here are four of the main ones: pivot, hinge, ball and socket, and one with a funny name – ellipsoid.

If you keep your body still but can swivel your head, you are using a pivot joint.

Ellipsoid joint

Pivot joint

Hinge joint

Try waving. Ellipsoid joints allow hands to move from side to side, forward and backwards.

Can you bend your knees and sit down? Hinge joints at your knees make this happen.

Ball and socket joint

I can't Hula Hoop well but if I pretend to, I'm able to move my pelvis in a circle due to ball and socket joints at my hips. Can you pretend to Hula Hoop?

VERTEBRAE

Ever wondered what those knobbly bits are running down your back? Let me introduce the spinal column: a collection of 33 bones called vertebrae.

The spinal column protects delicate nerves (the spinal cord) that connect all of the parts of the body to the brain. It is also like scaffolding for our upper body.

Your head is connected to the rest of the spinal column by seven vertebrae in your neck called the cervical spine (in yellow).

The sticky-out bit at the base of your neck is usually part of cervical vertebrae seven – can you find yours?

The thoracic spine (in pink) has twelve vertebrae that connect to our back ribs.

Amazingly humans and giraffes both have seven neck vertebrue – a giraffe's are just longer!

The lumbar spine (in green) has five vertebrae and attaches our chest to our pelvis.

Coccyx bones aren't much use to humans today, but in other mammals they form their tail!

The sacrum bone (in purple) is five vertebrae fused together. It looks like a shield!

The coccyx bone (in blue) is usually formed of four small vertebrae fused together.

MOVING MUSCLES

Muscles are made of fibres that stretch and pull to produce movement. Can you guess what your strongest muscle is? It's the masseter! Clench your teeth together hard and feel just under your cheeks – the lumps are masseters. They help us open and close our mouths.

Muscles have so many functions: they help us move, breathe, swallow, see, talk, poo, wee, digest food and direct blood to different parts of our body. Wow!

The fastest muscle is the orbicularis oculi. There is one around each eye. They can snap our eyes shut in one tenth of a second!

There are about 600 muscles in your body. Muscles are made up of three main types:

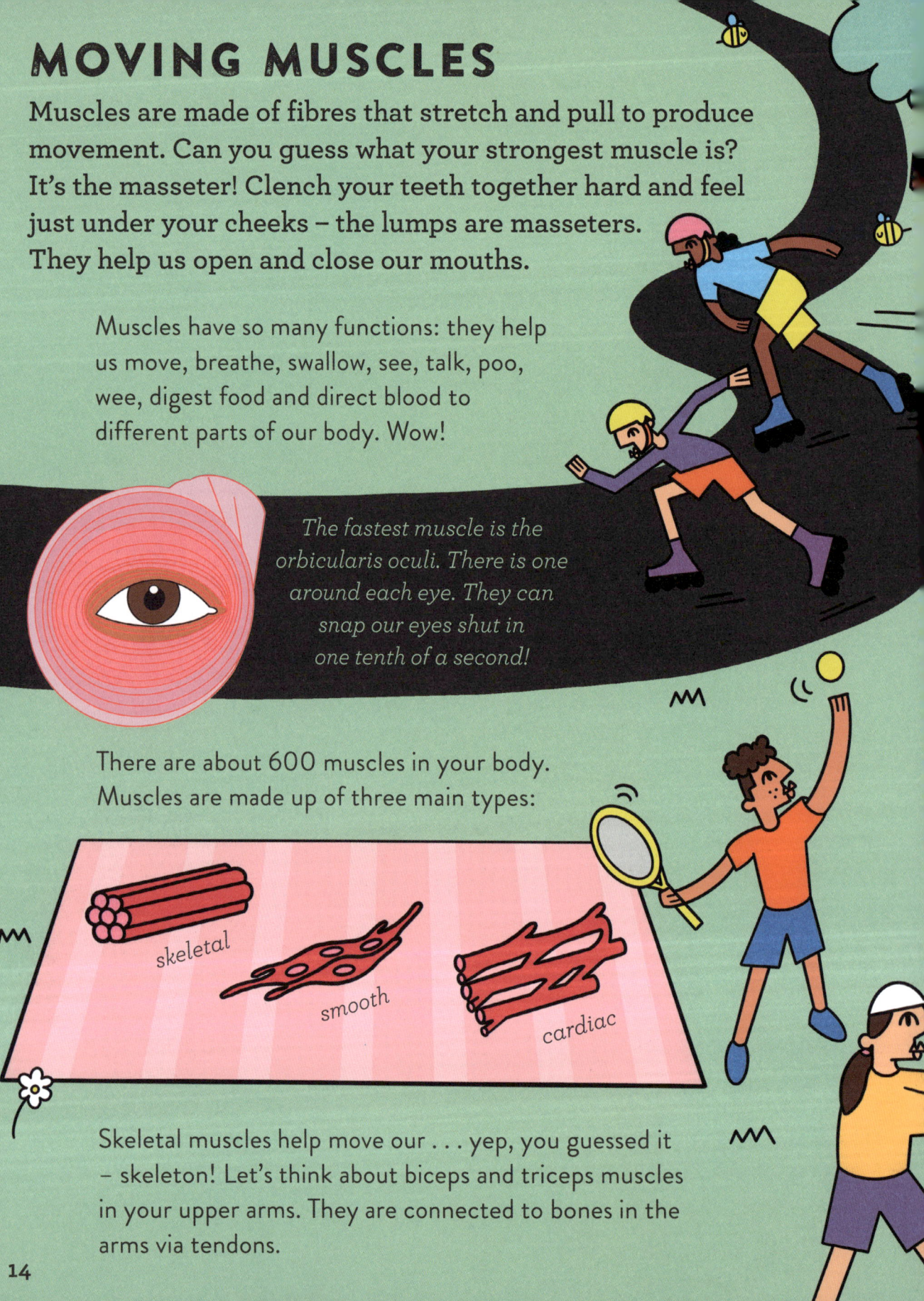

skeletal

smooth

cardiac

Skeletal muscles help move our . . . yep, you guessed it – skeleton! Let's think about biceps and triceps muscles in your upper arms. They are connected to bones in the arms via tendons.

When you want to bend an arm, your brain sends signals to your biceps via nerves. The muscle fibres then get shorter (contract) and pull on tendons. When you want to straighten an arm, the biceps relaxes (and the triceps contracts).

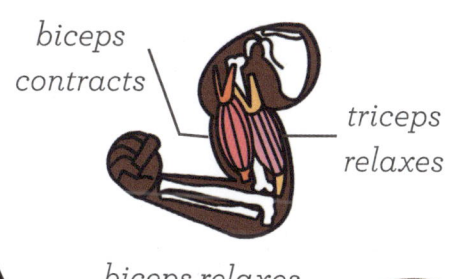

biceps contracts

triceps relaxes

biceps relaxes

triceps contracts

Smooth muscle works without us thinking about it. Clever! In our gut it helps push food along as each area of smooth muscle contracts and relaxes. And in the walls of our bladder it helps us control our wee. Phew!

The largest muscle is the gluteus maximus. It makes up the bum muscle!

The smallest muscle is in your ear. It's called the stapedius and is less than 2 millimetres long.

Cardiac muscle is my favourite because it is only found in the heart. Its main job is to pump blood around our bodies.

PUMPING BLOOD

I think the most magical thing about the heart is that it beats without us needing to think about it. As you read this, your heart is pumping blood all around your body!

Your heart sits just left of the centre of your chest. It is so powerful that if you trace a finger down the palm side of your thumb and stop about two centimetres below the crease of your wrist, you can feel your pulse – this represents your heart pumping.

Blood travels around your body via blood vessels (tubes called veins and arteries). These networks of tubes resemble tree branches.

It takes about 20 seconds for blood to flow around the body once.

In an average lifetime the heart will beat over 2.5 billion times.

If you joined all of your blood vessels together, they could go around the world more than once!

Valves in the heart stop blood flowing in the wrong direction.

To the left lung

To the right lung

To the heart

To the heart

Pulmonary artery

Pulmonary vein

Pulmonary artery

Pulmonary vein

Aorta

Superior vena cava

Left side of the heart

Right side of the heart

Valves

The thickest part of the heart is on the left side. This is because it needs to be strong enough to push blood all the way down to your toes!

The aorta's main purpose is to carry blood and oxygen to the whole body. The aorta divides into smaller arteries.

The aorta is the largest blood vessel – up to 30 centimetres long and 2.5 centimetres wide. Grab a ruler to see its size!

Aorta

To the rest of the body

Back to the heart

Inferior vena cava

The heart is divided into two sides: left and right. Both pump at the same time but to different body parts. The right pumps blood to the lungs where it joins with oxygen. The left pumps blood and oxygen to the rest of the body – so clever, don't you think?

Can you make a fist with your hand? That's about the size of your heart. But don't worry, as you grow, your fist gets bigger and so does your heart!

The superior vena cava and inferior vena cava are large veins that take blood that contains almost no oxygen from the body back to the heart.

THE STRONG SKULL

The skull by itself can look pretty scary, right? But try to think of the skull as scaffolding of the face. The 22 bones in an adult skull come together like a jigsaw and form the structure of our faces.

Eye socket

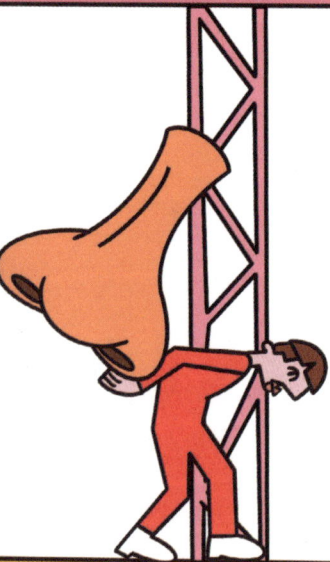

Noses are shaped by hard bone and squishy cartilage. Run your finger from between your eyes to the tip of your nose to feel bone and then cartilage. Cartilage is useful because we can squeeze our nostrils to keep out yucky smells!

Teeth

I bet you didn't know that the lower jaw where your bottom teeth sit is the only bone in an adult's skull not locked in place. It connects to your skull by a sliding hinge joint.

Place a finger where your ear lobe joins your face, and open and close your mouth. This is the joint working.

A baby has a massive skull compared to their body. They are born with a skull that is in nearly 40 pieces; most of it fuses together by about 18 months old.

Skull

Ears are shaped by cartilage, too. Everyone's ears have their own special shape and even the two ears that we each have aren't identical!

The bones that make up the skull help keep your brain safe from the outside world.

Spinal cord

The skull has many openings that allow nerves to connect with the rest of the body. The biggest opening is at the base of the skull where the spinal cord travels.

19

THE CONTROL CENTRE

On the outside, the brain looks like a wibbly, wobbly, wrinkly, boring, grey lump. But it's actually the body's supercomputer. It can help us move, eat, store memories, remember things we have learned, and imagine things.

The brain has three major parts: the cerebrum, the cerebellum and the brainstem. The cerebrum is divided into lobes that control different activities.

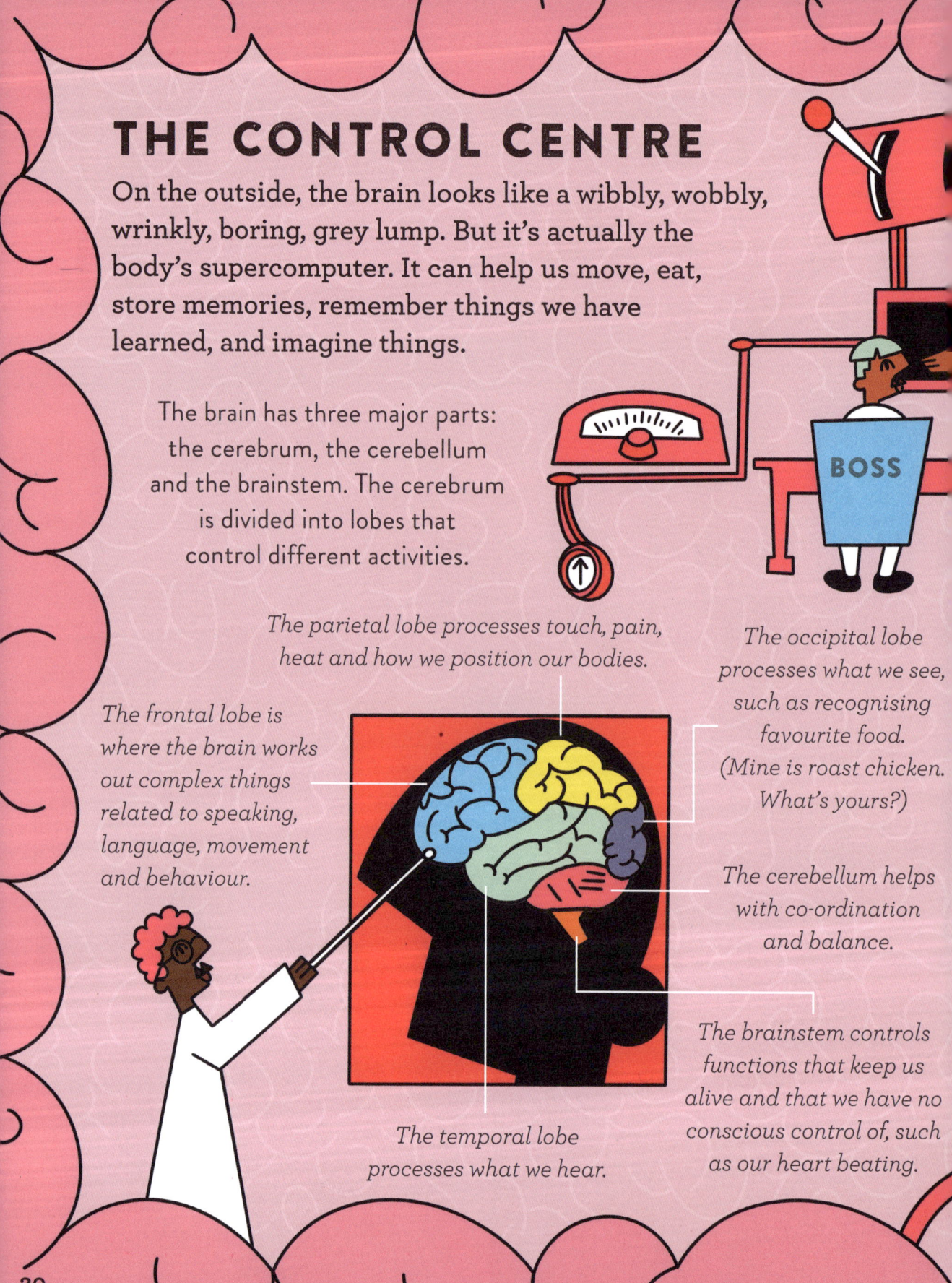

BOSS

The parietal lobe processes touch, pain, heat and how we position our bodies.

The occipital lobe processes what we see, such as recognising favourite food. (Mine is roast chicken. What's yours?)

The frontal lobe is where the brain works out complex things related to speaking, language, movement and behaviour.

The cerebellum helps with co-ordination and balance.

The brainstem controls functions that keep us alive and that we have no conscious control of, such as our heart beating.

The temporal lobe processes what we hear.

How does your brain tell your body what to do? How do your feet, which are so far away from your brain, know when to move? This is where nerve cells come in!

Movement nerve cells help move parts of our body (such as feet), and sensory nerve cells help us work out taste, touch, smell, vision, balance and noise. Connection nerve cells link two nerve cells together.

BOSS

BOSS

I think of nerve cells as cables, carrying electrical impulses of information to and from the brain. Nerves run to and from most parts of our body, have different functions and carry SO much information.

To me, a typical nerve cell looks like an upside-down tree!

The longest nerve is the sciatic nerve. It runs from the lower spine, into your bottom, down the back of your leg, to the heel of your foot!

HOW WE BREATHE

As you read this book, you would have taken about 12 breaths a minute. But what is the point in breathing? Well, the air around us contains oxygen and our body uses oxygen to turn food into energy. We need energy to function and grow!

We use our respiratory system to take in oxygen from the air and breathe out waste gases, such as carbon dioxide. Let me tell you how this works . . .

Our brain sends signals via nerves that cause us to take a breath in via our mouth and nose. Air containing oxygen travels down our windpipe, which divides into smaller tubes called bronchi and then into even smaller tubes called bronchioles. At the end of the bronchioles are alveoli. Oxygen moves through the walls of the alveoli into our blood.

Air then moves into our lungs, which sit inside the ribs and on top of a muscle called the diaphragm.

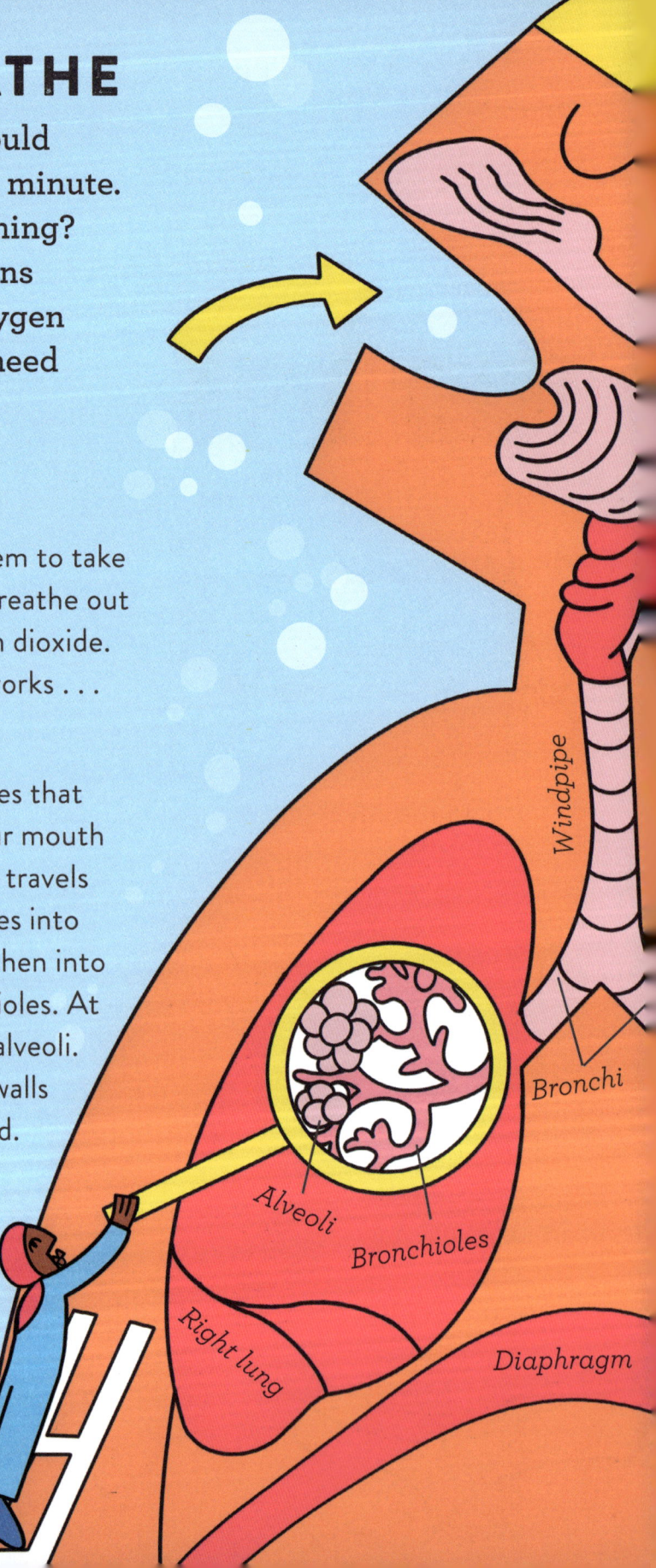

Windpipe

Bronchi

Alveoli

Bronchioles

Right lung

Diaphragm

We breathe in and out about 22,000 times a day!

When you do activities that need more movement, your body needs more oxygen (to help the body produce energy from food). So when you are moving fast your breathing will be quicker!

Take in a deep breath. You will feel your ribs move up and out – thanks to the rib muscles contracting. Your diaphragm also contracts and flattens down to make space for your lungs to fill with oxygen.

Now breathe out. The ribs move down because your rib muscles relax. The diaphragm also relaxes, helping squeeze air containing waste gases out of the lungs.

Left lung

The left lung is actually smaller than the right, as the left lung has to make space for the heart.

Lungs can be compared to balloons. They are almost round when full of air and collapse down and are flatter when the air leaves.

WEE WEE

Most people don't know where their kidneys are but let me tell you a trick to help. Put your hands on your hips. Well, where your thumbs are, is where your two kidneys are!

Our kidneys are the body's washing machine – they remove waste products from the blood and create urine (a doctor's term for wee!).

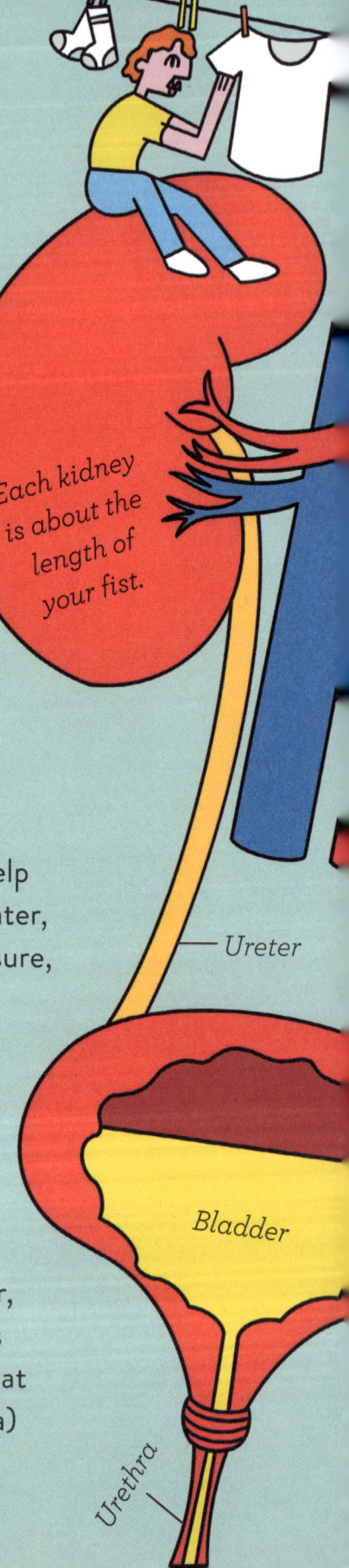

Each kidney is about the length of your fist.

We have two kidneys but our remarkable human body can function with just one.

You have probably guessed that the kidneys have other jobs too. They help our body maintain the right amount of water, release hormones that control blood pressure, AND help us use vitamin D to keep bones strong and healthy.

VITA MIN D

How do kidneys help us pee? Well, a tube (ureter) takes waste products (urine) from each kidney to the bladder, where it is stored. When the bladder is about half full, the brain sends signals that you need to pee. Another tube (urethra) allows urine to flow out of your body.

Ureter

Bladder

Urethra

blood vessels

You can tell a lot about how well hydrated you are by the colour of your wee. Wee should be light yellow.

What colour is your wee today?

GREAT

NOT GREAT

In the past (before clever tests were invented), doctors used to smell and taste wee to diagnose some illnesses – gross right, I would never have done this!

Funnily enough, kidneys look like kidney beans!

RED WEE AND SMELLY WEE!

Your urine will turn red for a while if you eat lots of beetroot. Don't be alarmed, you're OK. This happens because the kidneys have filtered out red pigment from the beetroot you don't need, into your urine.

If you eat asparagus, your urine will have a funny smell. This is due to gases produced by bacteria.

POO POO

Poo is my favourite subject. Don't be shy, everybody poos, but how does the body make it and WHY IS IT SO SMELLY?

Poo (I should say faeces because that's the scientific term!) starts off as the food we eat, which travels down our oesophagus and into our stomach. To stop food going into our lungs there is a flap (epiglottis) at the back of our throats, which covers our windpipe.

Oesophagus

Food is broken down by acid and digestive juices in the stomach, and churned around. The mushed-up food now has a new name: chyme. It then moves into the small intestine.

Only a small number of people can see the epiglottis when they open their mouth wide. I am one of them, are you?

Small intestine

Most of the useful nutrients in what we eat are absorbed from chyme in the small intestine.

If stretched out, an adult small intestine would be about seven metres long.

The gall bladder squeezes a green liquid (bile), into the small intestine. Bile is made in the liver and helps break down fat in the chyme.

Liver

Gall bladder

Pancreas

Chyme travels through the long, narrow small intestine by peristalsis. Ok, let me explain. Have you seen how a worm moves? That's kind of how chyme moves. Muscles in the small intestine contract and relax to push chyme to the shorter, thicker large intestine.

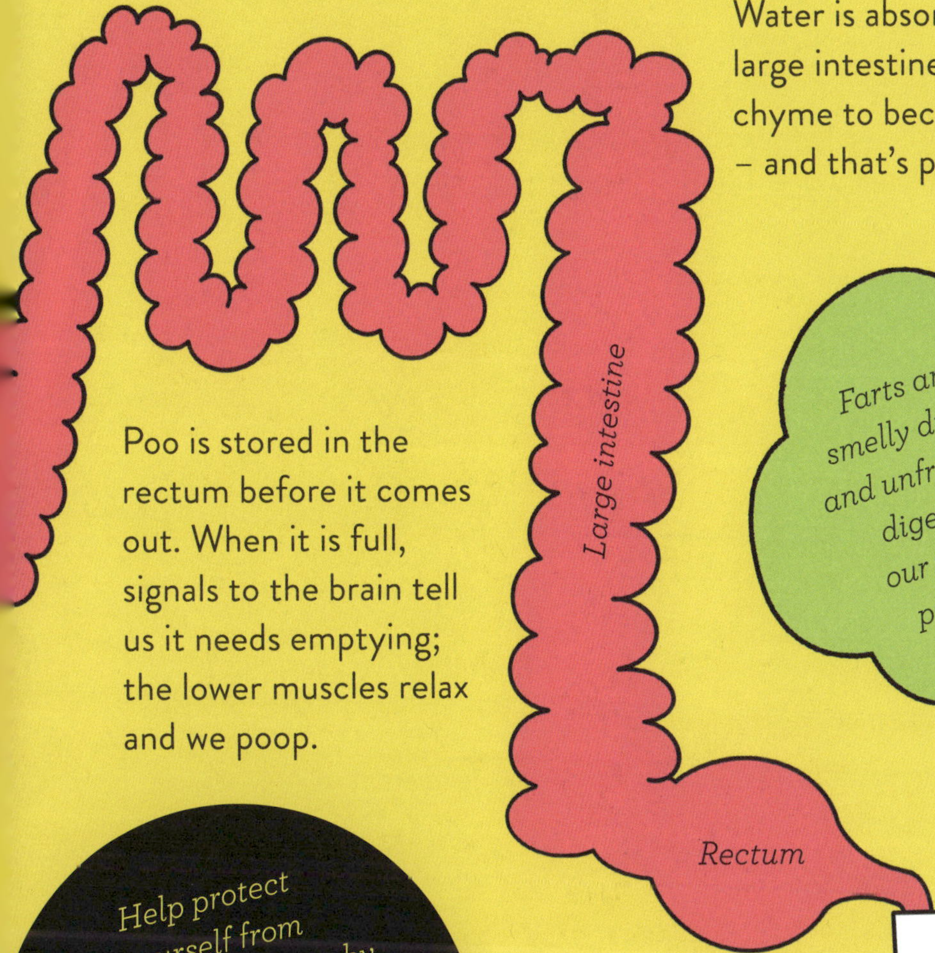

Water is absorbed in the large intestine, causing chyme to become harder – and that's poo!

Poo is stored in the rectum before it comes out. When it is full, signals to the brain tell us it needs emptying; the lower muscles relax and we poop.

Large intestine

Farts and poo are smelly due to friendly and unfriendly bacteria digesting food in our intestines and producing gas.

Rectum

Help protect yourself from unfriendly bacteria by washing hands with soap and water for at least 20 seconds, especially after using the toilet and before eating.

So there we have it, Dr Ronx's tour of the human body! Your brain must be bursting with information and I bet you can't wait to share what you've learned. So that's mission completed for me, you are now a Little Expert!

EXPERT!

GLOSSARY

bacteria – Teeny tiny organisms that can be found virtually everywhere. Some are harmful and some are useful.

---

cartilage – Strong, flexible tissue that absorbs shocks throughout the body (kind of like a cushion) and protects bones.

---

cells – The building blocks of life. The human body is made up of trillions of different cells that keep it working.

---

hormones – Chemicals that travel in our blood and tell processes in our body to start, speed up, slow down and stop, like little messengers.

---

ligaments – Strips of strong tissue that keep bones together at joints to help you move around and support muscles.

---

liver – I like to think of the body's largest organ as the blood cleaner. The liver breaks down medicines to help them work, breaks down harmful chemicals and helps create nutrients that the body needs.

---

minerals – Chemicals, such as calcium, iron and potassium, that the human body needs in very small amounts to stay healthy.

---

nutrients – Substances that help us survive and grow, such as water, vitamins, minerals and protein.

---

oxygen – A chemical element, found naturally in the air, that we need to survive. It provides energy so our bodies can function.

pancreas – An organ that produces hormones and other chemicals to help with digestion and control the amount of sugar in our blood.

---

respiratory system – Parts of the body that work together to help us breathe in oxygen and breathe out waste products such as carbon dioxide.

---

tendons – Strong and flexible tissue that connects muscles to bones.

About the Author
Dr Ronx is an award-winning trans non-binary emergency medicine doctor, TV presenter and loveable loudmouth with an unwavering desire to be the representation that young people need to see more of. This is their first ever book. #youcannotbewhatyoudonotsee

About the Illustrator
Ashton Attzs is a UK-based artist. Attzs' paintings and digital illustrations are a vehicle to empower and celebrate the everyday person.